THE LUST OF LIFE

SANDEEP DAHIYA

For all the lusty lovers of life!

Contents

Contents

Contents

Foreword

Plato: "Every heart sings a song, incomplete, until another heart whispers back. Those who wish to sing always find a song. At the touch of a lover, everyone becomes a poet."

And as love caresses you, you are supposed to turn a poet. And your life a poem. A life lived poetically nourishes your soul. The prose approach to life is simply to earn the conveniences to support you materially.

Niels Bohr, lost in the endless evolution of atomic possibilities at the subatomic level, surrendered his hardcore matter of factuality and turned a dreamer: "When it comes to atoms, language can be used only as in poetry. The poet, too, is not nearly so concerned with describing facts as with creating images."

If life appears stale and boring, you have got to blame your own self. For you lack imagination in not seeing the endless colors and splendorous charms lying around.

A bit of poetic daydreaming detoxifies the crammed brain because with poetic imagination, a sense of beauty pervades your being, putting all other pinching realities of life at bay.

You have got to believe me, the Big Bang was a poetic moment. If not for the infinite possibility of rhyme and rhythm, me and all you out there won't have been enjoying this beautiful unfolding of things and phenomena according to self-sustaining laws.

Without the seed of poetry there won't be any prose. Just like without the tiny seed there won't be a tree. The canopy, the full foliage of the tree, is just an extension of the dream lying with its realistic potential inside the small seed. The elaborate network of trunks, branches, twigs, flowers, fruits and leaves is nothing but a commentary on the small poetic seed. So all ye wannabe writers of a good life story, nurture the poet in you, who understands the value of pause in life, who moves slowly to watch everything, sight and smell everything. Whose senses are open to the inclusive interplay of wonderful harmonies of the supreme song, the universe, *the one song.*

The brushstrokes of poetry softly touch the soul without disrupting its restful muse and bring out the nuggets of love, compassion, harmony and peace. If you are poetic in nature, you have the potential to be anything because all these elaborate extensions of your life, your dreams, your professional and personal goals, your milestones, the world around you, all these and more are nothing but a reflection of that poetic pure seed.

Being poetic is being the master of all the best-ever possible emotions as a human being. No wonder love and poetry are almost synonymous. Poetry is the common soul of all the art forms. It's a smiling and loving approach to life, not just rhymes on paper. It's about being in tune with the soft chimes of your soul. It is impossible to visualize an unpoetic artist. It's impossible to have an unpoetic visionary. It's impossible to have an achiever who did not dream poetically.

Poetry is the womb that mothers all that has ever been loved and appreciated by the mankind and Mother Nature. To be poetic is to love. You taste godliness by being poetic. The mankind has pictured heaven just as a huge poetic dream. All the myths, gods and goddesses are marvelous poet philosophers and poet soldiers. So learn to be a poet. Love yourself as a poet. You will find love shielding you with its soft power making you the best of a human being.

Irony is that our language is a poor carrier of the ultimate truth. But ultimate truth is best summarized by the word 'love'. Within written styles, poetry lets loose its open invitation to invite truth. Even though it smiles hazily, yet it has its charms; some poetic outpour to reach out to the ultimate with your love.

1. Flirtations with Life

Here I come to this small puddle,
Sit on its shore and feel water,
Scorching sun, wind hot, dust fly,
Oasis driven, I but ogle at the water only.
Boiling pot it seems; vapourising layers,
Few lives drop in it suddenly:
Sparrows few wet feathers there,
Lifefully they escape the rising dead water.
With my feet in water and
Chin domed upon hands beaming knees,
I see life flirting in dying water,
Skin hard, meanwhile, feels molecules going up.
'Life is here or there?' I think,
Mirages over ponderous small waves,
Oh Yes! Water dies but plays still;–
Flirt we have with life; death weds in the end.

2. That Unknown Place

Some deep forest it was somewhere;–
Oak, ash, elm, beech, sycamore,
Embracing, climbing vines dare
Heights where love opened door.
There love need not be made,
Rather it existed stoically,
And not as desire's aid;
Stepped it out naturally, not frolically.
There leaves shone full green,
And grew pale after youth's bloom,
Floated then downwards unseen,
Ha! O death, thy own doom!
The place, creator of its own destiny:
Accident, predetermination there fail,
Basks timeliness of instants many!
Wonder, whether they ever caught time's tail?
Silent to the very core of silence,
Save some silent symphony by
Some bird larking by some unknown sense;
Noise of every sort there die.
Too unfamiliar a place,
Even to the sun partially known,
Curiously, thus, passes its face,

Doubting its fatherhood own.
Cloud crops fall into a world;
A world which its geography fathom not,
And in rumble-tumble they get rolled
Without hurt; Aaha! Cradle-caught.
The place where past seemed so evident,
Still present so independent!
And future with much secure accent,
Heavens! None from the trio lost with head bent.
Distance found itself unitless
Before the spread of that place;
Who can measure utter bliss?
Greenery that perplexed its face.
It looked as the centre of all goodness on earth;
As if God Himself comes there sometimes,
And rejuvenate all that mirth,
Persists which there as heavenly rhymes.

3. Flower when thou did not know thyself as such; I saw thy beauty bloom much.

I watched a flower since birth,
Then a small plantlet greenish,
Whom eyes won't distinguish
From the myriads born on the earth.
Grew it thus on its own mirth,
And devoid of any coronary wish,
Arose it then only affectionate kiss;
What a free hand for beauty's birth!
Afterwards, I saw it budding;
Beauty which earlier knew itself not,
Got now aware of its budding heaviness,
And once small hatchling,
Stood, now, proud for flowery shot
By those full scented petals fresh.

4. Whose Success are You Going to Feast Today?

O sweet success, fragrance of nectar,
So many flowery moments got
Themselves killed for these clappings far,
Wined throats now celebrate a lot.
Suppose the flowers had lost for vain,
And bad fumes cometh out of the passioned flame,
That single bent head had bore pain,
Too many pocked noses had sought blame.
Aye! What one standth to lose or gain?
From the mob which gulps only by the name;–
Benumbed by victory; failure maketh insane;
One's abhorred content changed there to lusty fame.
Thus the story of success-failure goes,
Prickles too many for a single rose.

5. The Saviour

He fell violently in love;
Big, stormy, illusionary ripples got a love-wreck,
And like life's instinct when death doth attack
Only her image waved around him now.
In such a storm only the heart doth row,
While poor mind fell off the deck;
Logic struggled for its life behind back,
And storm intoxicated heart throbbed upon bow.
Logic but is such a slave;
Struggled it for a 'follow'.
And storm when subsided to show the captain's
Loss of direction; whom to look for a save?
Fortunately, mind stood there with a glow,
Saved, thus, from further delusionary pains.

6. Immortal Beauties

When I think about the past,
Time's load overcast
Rumbling clouds stretching vast,
So many beautiful things died; now aghast
Me remember them as alive for the last,
Alas, but life is so fast;
So many beauties annihilated in the merciless blast.
At each step a graveyard,
Present's efforts fought hard;
Like versified truth from some bard;
Then coffin cradled, which once flowered
And whom this hasty runner favoured,
Now when time hath devoured,
Me prepare its next food; step as forward.
How impermanent, transient is life!
So many full flowers cuts time's knife,
Still at each futuristic step we arrive
At something where newborns thrive,
And for more and more we strive,
Alas but, sacrificial presents only for the past's survive,
And future's tiny, trivial, momentous drive.
Are those graved beautiful flowers dead?
Whom no eye would ever read,

No! Seeds they are which time had
Furrowed along a path by someone who bravely lead,
Bloom they will again afore some eyes sad,
Whose present-past coexist and future dead,
My graved beauties then'll relive afore that bent head.
His senses lying rusting,
Still something in the dust goes bursting;
Swelling to Himalayan husting,
While illusion's death hissing;
Dying before newborn rising
Above father's head, where Gods watch praising.

7. Glimpses of Something about Love

Where the light shines to the last ray
And night falls prey
Upon the rugged day
Sprawled mountains array.
And it raining to day's last grey,
Drops shower darkness to lay
Solitude in night's fray,
While the clouds thickening make way
For drunken wet night, which say
Like a drenched damsel makes hay:
'See me not, for I foray
Hilarious hug in lover's shrug, Oye!'
Vow, that eagerness! Sea ye
Seemst dying to see off the day,
Thy quivering pout through bay
Excites earth to foreplay;
Closing eyes to gentle breezy sway.
Alas! Eyes, imagination goes nay,
And the love scene blurs away,
Her sprawled hair put shadowy sway.

8. Love Someone's Life Flower

Life, how much should I love thee?
And in which form and appearance?
Is it the one inside me
Or, the heart's praise for that flower with fragrance?
The flower possessed by fear,
Love it is, or owner's craze?
While, wildlife throbbing near,
And the flower still uncaught by
Someone's love-net's maze.
Why must a flower be loved?
Is it that it appears beautiful?
Or, love it creates which moved
An inward passion from death's pull.
O thou flower, I love thee more than the self,
For thou art the dreamy life unpossessed.

9. Immortal Daughter

Ye black clouds amidst
Dark night knowst not,
How thy smallest daughter kisst
Slightest opening in bud's pout.
Flower's cherub and thine,
And sissy, hilarious time's twin,
Thou seest not thy rhyme,
Pass thundering, lightening wink.
Huge! Thou dost overcast sky;
Time also takes mountainous leaps;
And flowers stretch heavenly eye,–
Thou three infinite parents.
Still, three children thine,
Only through them thy worth shine.

10. Duty to the Beauty

These tiniest showers fall,
Just like dream sweetest call
When we lie asleep,
Beloved, thy same slender sip
Through eyes leaves me wined;
As if in heavens I dined.
Those pouty fishy full lips;
Divine experience smitten tips,
And me smooched over them,
Plucked, then, the sweetest gem
Out of feminine treasure house,
Oh! Greatest fire it dost douse.
And thou fall for me
Like the windfallen flower to see
Its beauty fully blown;
Those petals having much shone,
Now was the time
To reach the prime.
O my beauty, I am the means to thy end,
Thou art Godsent,
And me the beauty's supplement;
To be used for its fulfillment,–
Black bee for the bud virgin,

Beauty's utility then begin.
What a great utilitarian, beauty!
So many boulders haughty
Corrode to die a death sandy,
So that river's curves become more trendy,
Flows which then with a pride;
Starry eyes shine, O groomed bride.
I'm made for thee sweetlet,
Damn sure, I can bet
To exist away from company thine,
Thou but can't without this pine,
And some say I consumeth you,
Me thus the blamers sue.
O my little flower, tell
Me a single one dwell
Immortal in this world
Without crusher's press hurled
Around the petals soft,
While the perfume cometh
As the much cherished croft.
I exist for thee, O my beauty,
'Complete thou' is my duty.

11. An Orphan (or half orphan) in the Night

O child, where thy mother hast gone?
Standth as thou in this dark night,
Tears thy go waste; succeeds only moan,
Where ist thy absolute right to sleep quiet?
That mother, who shines as some distant star,
I doubt that she is too far;
Too away is the smiley spark to mar
The ghosts, and encourage thy tiny soul at war.
O thou two unfortunate ones,
Slept when together, time was once,
Now but both awake,
Why doesn't she take thee away and make
A little star near her for thy sake,
So that cry thou not
and motherhood drown in sorrowful lake.

12. When Time was Helpless before You

Thou art beauty unchanged, unmoved
Just like that waterfall always the same;
Whose persistence running water can't tame,–
That gracious continuity which time always pursued.
Thy gentle breezy state maketh time nude;
Attired if not by its changing game,
And thy beauty becometh a name;–
A picture which lives; never moved.
I salute thy infinite instantaneous beauty,
Thou smile and live for the beauty's sake;
A beauty that was and will remain forever,
Time's elements will try haughty,
But it can never take
So many jewels from thy lover.

13. One Simple, Real Beauty

Country girl, I salute thee for thine rusticity;
That devoid of complexity, which
Bathes thee naturally without made-up artificiality,
Thou art only thou; not try to become such.
Least conscious about thy greatest gift,
Thou pour smile uninhibited,
Truth about thee never shift
Beneath thin layers venerated.
I like thee for what thou art,
Too little thou have to show other than thou,
Thy inner self and outer never part;
False seeds thou never sow.
Thou represent crystal clear beauty,
Thank God for thy farness from the city!

14. Far! Far! Somebody is in Need Let Me Soak Miseries All

Let my tear drop
Where there is hunger and pain
And too many a sandy grain
For a single drop of rain;
Where in eyes drained, hopes never prop,
Lord! Let my eyes give fullest crop!
For their slightest pain
Let my heart bloody drain
The terrain, where death grope.
Let that infant's puzzled look,–
Due to unholy experiences first–,
Cast gloom, pain over my face
For the childhood hanged by the hook,
Let me begone of my thirst!
Hold me back from the life's race.

15. Some Lines for Some Time in Future

When thy eyes begin to glow dimly
And walk form not a rhyme with the body;
Flowers when gone for a single lily
And world's eyes see not once fair lady;
When even cup loathes thy shaky pout
And time engraves its loath on thy rosy cheeks;
Eyelids drop when for vision out
And life only but leaks;
When thy grey hair die day by day
And all crests shrink to troughs;
See thou not when a single ray
And violently shake thee those coughs.
Then dear, pick my book up,–
Where thy youth shines immortally,
Unhampered by the time's hand rough.

16. Sister

O my dear sis,
Time was then all bliss,
This once home thine, now miss
All that growing, evolving care and wish
Thy sweet happy return
To the place where you were born.
Thou for a greater purpose gone
To nurture life in some home,
Still, thy place becomes a shrine here;
Down to dusk, work with so much care,
I can still sense thee in this air,
Circulates which orderly, like my sis fair.
Thy virtues sing, commit when we mistake,
Great are the homes whom sisters make.

17. Gypsy Girl

Like the mystical flower, seen here then there,
The lovely wild maiden, spring laden
Showst its non-periodic rare; not to care,
Stupefied eyes gaze but settlement ridden.
O flowery lass, thy breeze-driven gyrations
Prop winy drops upon tongues,
Still, thou unapproachable to focussed vibrations,
Through thy escapements caravan moves, singths.
How can thou be so heartless!
Not to fix eye somewhere for someone,
And always fly away without bestowing a single kiss!
What a classy heart to be won!
Gypsy girl, thou spread beauty's message:
Sudden full arrival, lost then in a haze.

18. Ode to the Spring

Labour is in the air around;
Spring sun fades the wheat green,
Their grainy tops; ripening and ageing;
Million crowns from the clown's kingdom,
Prepares as he for the labour duty.
Spring, the season of fruition, procreation,–
Nature's ejaculations for *kama-mahautsava*,
Now when cold father makest love to mother warm,
First cries of numerous infants chirp around;
Picturesque gift, merge as they in one:
Spring is here, mature and blown full.
What a great time it is;
New comers smile first; do they cry!?
Flowers wild, isolated, conceived hastily–
Nettle, clover, primrose, thistle–
Worry they not uncaring parents,
Who, too sensuous, flow blindly,
And these small daughters or sons
Scent the solitude, wilderness around,
Play they with hurrying swallow tails
And fear not moths in the dark,
Mature as if, welcome they bees.
More flowers than eatables around,

The season with the message:
'Reality lies in eyes, not mouth,'
New leaves, new colours, and hopes new,
Bunchgrass, weather beaten by the cold, relive new,
Reed warbler gets sinews new,
Hangs as it among lengthy stalks,
And nature lulls them through skylark's beak,
Seemst it if a virgin maiden
Sings, dances wildly like grassy 'wavy hair',
Would be mother!
Enters the conjugal threshold now.
What if one fade in, and the other fade out,
Colours emerging or going out care not,–
The days are just matchless,
Spring, the season balanced; the day and nights
Cool warmed, or warm cooled.
The landscape becomes a garden,
Lie where so many beauties;
Each and everything beautiful,
Need not they, thus, caring special,
Urge is just to create new,
While, spring tracks the parental escapades.
Now, when waters go heavens,
Except the dewy rain of nights;
Waterbodies—puddles to ponds—start slimming,
Slimming like a narrow curve around the back;
The back of springy damsel.

More are seekers now; drops becoming divine!
Thirst forces more walks over banks transitory.
Smallest grassy worlds, tiny flowers, insects
Anguish not the hierarchy above:
Spring flowering from man's to His kingdom,
Hides as the burying beetle; passes a foot near by.

19. Kisses of Now and Afore

Beloved, don't think that I'm
Speaking it out of ebriation;
Heart's depth wine can't fathom,
Only distilled souls scent gyration
Of body, heart; and her figurine
Moving, inspiring, cajoling for conception,
Which minds never normally design.
Oh! My unfaithful lover,
Me pine for thee as afore,
When thou flooded this heart with thy shower,
Whose wavering tinkles reached this mortal's core,
Mortal still I'm; yet immortal!
For thy love always kindles soul,
Sleep thou now amidst that bliss marital,
And slap me as only destiny's play foul.
Thy love lightly flickers still;
Thou adorn heart's treasure tree,
Me, but, on the verge of fall from the hill,
Still, during the fall pray I'll for thee.
Fate may qualify me as a lover failed,
Yet in defeat lies my greatest win,
For, my sweet failure destiny hast hailed

As the success of the Lord's grin.
My drunken selfless heart wishes
Thou all the best in thy new start!
Worry not for the 'meant to be ashes,'
Forget the kiss last and that falling apart,–
Now, thou lick sensuously for a cause,
And me left apart
Like the whisper of an unrequited prayer;
A dry wish that makest not any noise,
Thy voluptuous smacks sound liar;–
Lying to hide someone thou loved,
Who from destiny's path never moved.

20. When I Love Thee Most

Beloved, when thou shrink in my arms,
And put thy lips on my thumping heart,
I feel sucked to celestial charms,
While thy long hair, like jasmine flirt.
Aha that twist of thy slender body!
Creeps which immeasurable lengths,
Infinite I feel, O my great lady,
Time's measure lost; a second worth months!
Those wide voluptuous eyes closing
And parting somewhat betwix eyelids,
For other world they are opening;
In that fainting look heaven glides.
Still, I love thee not for such forgetfulness,
I do, of course, when remember thy bodylessness.

21. O My Partner, thou art Beautiful than a Flower

April hast it, thus love springths;
For, whatever nature has to offer,–
Perfume! Flower crushed to suffer,
Vow! beauty's oozes man bringths.
Tryst further; driplets for love draught,
Sprinkles the petals sacrificed on body fairer,
Which lusty lips lick from the bearer,
Ha! Tasty tongue now sought
The beauty which eyes once praised.
And the love processor from nature
Eyes many more bounties on offer:
New names for beauties bruised,–
Transformations new for the love cure:
More love licks from the graved door.

22. My Fair Lady

Whenever stars start to fade,
And light seemst too far:
Too far to even shade
The dreams; as dark launches war.
Lightless, me comest across a cry:
'For dimming light's sake,
Please, go along and try
With smallest rays eyes make'.
Eyes, of course, where smallest
Sun shine in the middle,
Whom salty sea swallows:
Reflective more; solve riddle.
What if success embraces not,
And failure kisses many times,
Still, that smallest dot
Makest dark lady's passioned rhymes.
O my sensuous dark lady,
Sip thou the nectar of toil:
Thy consenting embrace always ready,
Ye succeed to love, help me fail.
Ye crazy infatuated lover,
Thank smallest twinkle in my eye,
Urges which to try forever,

Makest thee my sweet ally.
'Success', the other lady thou abhor,
Keep thy love thus secure day and night,
And thy lover knocking at her door,
While, thy embrace squeeze with more might.
O my fair lady, worry not,
She now fades away quickly more,
While, thou makest best with nuptial knot,
Urges she in a hasty cry, 'Again try, once more'.

23. Rainbowed Forehead

Optical phenomena in the sky,
The rainbow with spectrum colours,
I have my own on my forehead,
If they say space is infinite,
Contemplation ours can realise which,
Then my forehead is the same;
Like a sky after heavy shower,
Rain of struggle with reality,
And glimpses it when,
Just like a sun,
The arc of light shines,
Refraction of divine light on ideas mine,
The rain of ideas,
Just like falling water drops
Come in contact with the reality,
Deflect then to the unknown,
Never, never to return again.
Leave they coloured reality,
Colours seven showing the real,
Left I am with a rainbow
Arching across forehead mine,
Traces coloured of my encounter
With reality crowning forehead,

Worry I not failure with reality,
For coloured sparks I have got,
And a rainbow on my forehead!

24. Bridal Gifts from the Maiden

Lo earthlings, heaven was never so near!
Indra's thunderbolt enlighten and clouds cheer,
Child bride of yore;
Young lass returns for the marital bliss;
Aha! The rain returns to kiss
Forlorn, hot sighing partner ruing summer long,
Who out of excited warmth singths a song;–
First monsoon rain comes jangling,
Musical arrival upon the leaves swaying;
Small dances, embracing in dust still praying,–
'Come! Come! Can't bear more frying'.
Universal harmony pours upon mortals,
Many buds are here, awaiting to open petals:
See! Country maiden gone all wet,
Her heart thunder under her bosom to let
Loose, attire's control sticking around,
Also, the social constraints squeeze and bound,
Thank thee O rain! She overcomes the latter,
Gyrates to see her contours natural; no bloater,
While, drops almost mate around her full fishy lips,
So many, of course, mischievously pat upon shaking hips.
O lone outsider with thy cattle herd,

Thank thy local deity for being heard,
Thou look so rainy in those shaggy clothes;
Suck up so much water to desert's loathes,
Look at the reach of falling rain,
Even the hardest horns feel some lovely pain!
And they shut mouthed, stoically muse over the rare
Rain, which shrinks from the native land, as if not dare,
Then a sad reflection by closing heavy eyelids:
'Gets my village same big drops, or not?'
Birds still flutter around to chill,
Rain is hurtling down for life; not to kill,
Cares not the smallest world disaster floods,
Sacrifices it for cause greater, and no bloods,
Children run naked in the streets,
So many playmates fall with greets,
The rain is falling to rejuvenate again
Some sparkling in oldest eye for another begin,
Yes! First monsoonal harp is at our doorsteps,
Visible become as our footsteps.

25. Pa's Flower Bed

Some flowers have grown,
Watch as my father's eyes
Like fairies from the skies,
They glimpse his perfection; full blown,
Originated like earth; few seeds thrown,
Life hovers there, now, as butterflies:
Ecstasies on petals and good byes,
And his Godly muse over the beauty flown.
Father theirs, caresses bud each,
Expecting their arrival time, worried
Pours he dewy drops of smallest size,
And gentlest they sway with daughterly reach.
He ponders like the sun; they get energised,
Together even in dreamy nights, and then arise!

26. Hearty Flights over Our Heads

O birds! Thine world is fantastic,
Feathered tails, plumes ornamental,
Thine forelimbs modified as feathers,
Bones hollow, jaws elongated to bills,
Keel shaped breast bones make fliers strong,
Thou colonize different habitats:
Terrestrial, freshwater, marine.
Humanity's flying colours thou are,
Be it the cooing call from the dove,
Plumage soft, small headed female;
The lark singing through its bill slender,
Making flying clarinet; singing,
Or the strong magpie fighting crows,
Female strong; the exotica winning.
Be it the swift sparrow, high speeded,
Scimitar shaped wings and thrusts;
Human's urge to fly high and high,
Robs eggs when intelligent jackdaw,
Shows it our nasty snatching moods,
Or heron seizing fish from the water's edge,
With body slim and legs longish,
Proves it our artificiality for the survival.

Wood pecker prising off bark, probing crevices,
Shows the labour sense trunked around,
Or the wren, small and swift,
Feeding on small insect flocks beneath bushes,
Realises it millions bushing for bread,
Kookaburra pouncing upon snakes, lizards,
Or birds of prey; hunters nocturnal,
Their strong hooked bills, clawed talons,
Airs high speed dives on targets.
Perform acrobatic display for females,
Feathers thine drop over our ladies' hats,
And of course game birds for hunting;
Plumes, pillow and duvet stuffings.
Birds! What if we emerge the winners?
Innocence thine is still greater;
Damage crops or foul buildings,
Thou air humanity's flying colours,
Birds! Thine world is fantastic.

27. Musicity from Lips, Fingers

Humans bray so many voices:
Hard talks and linguistic vocal chords,
Music but is His voice,
The sound organised
In melody, harmony, rhythm,
Fingers when touch string,
Banjo, violin, viola, harp,
Vibrate all with tones sequenced,
Lips when protrude and puff,
Clarinet, cornet, horn, tuba,
Wind changes to divine pitch,
Or be it thumping fingers
Upon cymbals, drums,
Or harmony from harmonium,
Music speaks language one,
Cultural relativity binds it not,
Thus folk and music classical,
Music gets itself done,
Involuntarily they sway to it,
The aborigines and the civilized,
Pious, pure, lyricisd moments those,
Leave they tension theirs'

In divine one of the strings;
Blow their passions inside
The Godly air escaping;
And beat out fists, fingers
Upon those surfaces musical.

28. Whom should I ask about her?

Shall I tell thee reality about a woman,–
It is exact opposite of what others of her species
Narrate to the hopeful man;
No other query gets such misses.
O thou woman,
Why ye misperceive thyself
Before the true heart of men?
It is, but, mischievous wink about the self.
Why thy court can't find judgement fair?
That statue claim not to see,
Why then cheat by thy eyes unfair?
Why only the lie makest thee glee.
Thus, let every man find his own answer,
Listen upside-down to the self teaser.

29. Where shall I make a home for you?

That little paradise in a small vale,
Where a joint family flowers,
Brightest buds open for the elders pale,
Where green sloppy pastures
Hold upper rocky chin firmly,
And big neighbouring trees give lease;–
Terrace only for the family,
Whiles they from theirs sloppily appease.
Paradise where a small brooklet
Sneaks childishly from the parent's flow,
And sky's paradise all set
To do anything for the terrestrial child's glow.
Dear, let only thou accompany me there,
Disturb as thou not the heavenly air.

30. Sand Grain and a Water Drop

O thou cattle herder,
What forces thy migration?
'Save life' instigate
And thou become a wanderer:
Exiled like a sandy grain,
Flew which too high
And far with an 'aye'!
Found not, but, rain!
Where ist thy family?
Sandy message they groan,
And thou quench thirst daily.
God made cattle for graze:
Easily, without haste,
Battered them, but, with dusty chaste,
Now, harvested stumps they erase,
Outsiders they feel,
Thus the hurried pace
In the land distant,
Abhors which, even, hot western brace,
Helpless, thou ponder over the emigrant's rent,–
Waterbodies too small;
Only the dried crofts for all.

How far have ye trodden?
Weight on thy feet
Looks if hoofs beat;
Heavy, wearied; seem broken,
Chin thou support on
The *lathi* standing faithfully along:
Cool companion thine,
Its fearful strike blown,
And they needn't its shine,
For the animal energy gone,–
Weakly they swing horn.
Urge the rains!
With thy lips more parched;
Personify thy cattle's soul nerd!
Pray which can't, only feel the pains;
Join thy family chorus!
O herder, leave them not,
Needy cry can make Him porous,
Sand grains forming 'need dot',
'Rain here or there,'
We also await it like thee,
Single drop falling makest glee.

31. Oh! I am in love again!

Ye people, who speak of love,
Long after the first one is done,
Ye only fool some dove:
Numerical love is but a fun.
Fun from the side one, or both,
Befooling for marriage or lust,
Justified by taking an oath,
Alas! First one was the pure most.
Cometh which by itself,
Others are but dragged,
First one fools itself,
Others befool to be begged.
The former one nothing knowst,
Later ones almost spy the host.

32. To the Indian Woman on the Stage

O Indian woman!
Ye familiarise world now,
Beauty, brain, grace bravo!
Jewel amongst jewels,
Diamond outside, or inside dwells,
Alone and aloof thou adorn the crown!
Ramp they call it there,
Thou walk thy rise;
Bodies theirs as man's prize,
Thine becomes our pride,
Answers theirs only worldwide,
Vow! Thine art from where?
Reveal they physique outside,
Thou bringst the unseen,
Invisible; O smiling queen!
The Indian fairy on the stage,
Million dreams brightly gaze
At the dreamy pair where the crowns ride.
Salute thee O conqueror!
Ye breakst bondage physical:
Realise the man historical,–
Beauty not only in curves,

Oozes also through deep nerves,
Thank thee O smiling mirror!
O solace to the billions
Amongst poverty, toil without rest,
Aastha thou come at last;–
The new daughter of India,
Burning as the only *diya*;
As if moon brighter by a trillion!
World now at thy feet,
Proud anklets jingle,
While the noise around mingle
In thy success cry;
Eyes thy never too dry,
And so many defeated; more to beat!

33. Pages of My Effort: Tryst with Heaviest Book with One Lined Pages

Nothing seemst to 'change'
Despite the rule much fabled:
Booked life: its page
Or pages left just one lined,–
'Trysts hard and fail,'
And me gost turning more,
Hoping to arrive at destiny's hail,
Alas but monotony roar!
Life mine with few weighty words,
Make these an iron rod;
Black, heavy for paged birds,–
Too weighty a single turn, O God!
Thus, huge efforts with each page,
Still, but, the familiar ones gaze.

34. Springy Songs from Far

Now when the spring comes,
Attired with floridity, sprouts
New leaves, greenery new,
Alas! Visitors but prepare to go:
Ducks, storks, wadders,
The wagtails and the cranes,
Spent who chilly winters here,
Prepare these now to go.
Beatles, bees and insects,
Make merry meanwhile,
Sing a song of farewell,
Their small hymns and flights,
Wish the goers a happy journey,
Prepare as they for distances far,
Woodpecker, wren, sparrow,
Along with natives other
Rejoice over fruits ripening,
O gipsy birds, mind not!
Spring here if not thine,
Waits it somewhere else too,
So fly thou strong birds,
Spring somewhere calls you,

Sings a welcoming song,
If the spring flowering here
Bells departure thine,
Waits it gazelle eyed somewhere too.

35. The Place where Time Doesn't Find Space

The sun is shining brightly,
And sky if never painted cloudy,
Tranquility arises so highly;
Aloof from any reversal tidy.
Everything without a hurry;–
Man, material contended, satisfied,
Relax for calmness to carry
Them away from hot pursuit which once tied.
Where hast that urgency gone?
Makest which time too small,
Single instant now run
Endlessly without a fall.
Who sayth time never varies?
And instances are all the same,
Now each duty-less unit
Carries on and on without a name.
Ageless they now become,
Those who share this silence,
What are few sips of rum?
Here time drunk loses sense.
Transience wails somewhere far,
As it can't hurry over here

To create same killer war;
The war which permanence fear.
Thus, the time gost on living,
Surviving without any rebirth,
And clock's hands stop circling,
Lo all watches without worth!
O God! Make places such
Inside our restlessly bumping hearts,
Calculations where don't matter much,
And soul where only happily flirts.

36. Bye, Bye …………, Far Away

I try to look at
Something far away,
But alas! Like a short chat
Discourses fall far away.
The wilderness strayed afore,
Trees, terrain obstruct the show,
Walled, blinded feel I before
Nature's spread; feel low.
With narrowed eyes
Me cast a pinching sight,
Lost it is but in skies;
Something far and above the flight.
One picture is above:
From that far to my back;
Other end eyes don't show,
Multi-coloured in between hack.
I gaze the one vaulting
Like the brow upon eye,
Below goes the sighting,
And the 'far' bidding one-sided bye.

37. Success Thou must not Carry Me; For I Myself Carry Failure

With every step, I add to my failure,
Walks it with me or destiny?
They say victory doth always lure,
But I doubt if there exist any.
Still I work forward,
At least for not getting failed,
How can victory pour reward
On someone whom destiny jailed?
And I have to go till my last fall,
These small tumbles make me look below,
Victory would've only made a call
From the sky to cajole a blind follow.
Thus I like my failure,
For there is a constant knock at my door.

38. Who Fuels Bad History?

Anger comes just like a cloud;
As if a shadow over the sky's head
Obstructing the light of reason.
And what do we under its spell?
Nothing but the reaction,
Which our present doesn't
Want as its wanton past.
Let me wonder not, why
We have'd such garbage in the past;
The loathsome part of the era gone,
Loomed when dark clouds
On human head and reason failed;
Red veins attacked when temples,
Butchered love messengers midway,
And ill advised machine then
Went on rampage; mechanics bad.
O anger, perpetual source of destructive machine,
Thou energise human mechanics
To move towards destruction,
O annihilative instinct, why thou exist?

39. Why I Love My Country?

O my country, how much I love thee?
Only swelling bosom can tell;
Head when held high and face glee,
Glitters when a diamond out of the shell.
Defeat mine fall worthless
Before thy single victorious step;
That tear in eyes winless
Begins to shine for the new born in thy lap.
Yes, Indians we are, just Indians,
Please, define us not,
Or you will counter definition billions;
So many turns for a single knot.
O my India, so large and spread out;
Extensive to humanity's all parameters,
Still comes across a single shout,
Which every nook corner hears.
Religions here flow river like,
Doing what'er is required naturally,
And people dip to turn Godlike,
Nothing ends, of course, even after forehead lily.
O my country, I simply love thee,
Asks me if somebody, why?

Reason any I can't see,
And if still tell, then I lie.
Still, O my country, love is love,
And one loves without reason,
Confident I am only of one vow;–
'Work tirelessly for the golden vision.'

40. Harvesting Girl

Harvesting girl, thy wheatish brow,
Thereupon shine the labour crops,
Receding furrows of wheat heat thee up,
And thy sickle becomes *shakti*.
Parched lips, work strain on sweating face,
Trickle which upon eyelids and dreams,
Keep heart O girl, prism they are,
Showing imagination-hued coloured hopes;
Hopes of a good harvest; home upstaged
Or groomed dreams about marriage.
The wheatish colour strewn around,
All eager to be cut short by thy hands,
And there thou move ahead leaving stumps,
Wiping occasionally brow thine;
Dreamt harvest go off with a swipe.
Real thou become for the reality one:
Look at the furrows swaying ahead,
Hot noon, flying pollens show them oblong,
And thou start slowly-slowly again,
Brow thine meanwhile glitters with sweat drops tiny.
Drops which fall upon thy eye shelters,
Beneath narrowed eyes due concentration hard,
Still sun reflects through them,

And rainbowed vision thou have.
How much to be finished? Worry thee not,
Lost again in a dream, O girl, thou mingle in gold,
Work as thou bent headed; pollens fall,
Seems it thou harvesting, give offerings,
Blessed such thou reach furrow end,
Tire not O girl, furrows lie at thy feet.
Small sand-swirl passes as by,
Leaves it thy hair more pollen stricken; wind furrowed,
O windy girl, now when the *loo* is forming,
And all are afraid of sandy gusts,
Thou, but, have fire more inside thee,
Hence listen thou not its voice around ears,
Thus defeated it passes to flutter those leaves far,
Now when sun is shining overhead,
Like a father feeling for his daughter,
Stays it there to avoid thy face directly.
Thou smell the smell of ripened gold,
Sweat scented body thine sources it,
Mingles it with the blowing hot air,
And the message spreads over the vast fields,
The message of hard work without complaint,
Makest it the golden wheat more so;
Inspires the lonely hands struggling across furrows;
Beats away the looming defeat,
Harvester! Thou art the only flower,
For the spring begone, and honeybee wandering.

Peasant girl, stand thou upright for some backrest,
And look around into wheatish wilderness,
Nobody is there except some heads
Bent before the furrows and sickled hands,
Feel not forlorn O golden girl,
For thou art the brightest grain,
See! Each lesser one is looking up to you,
Become their role model for brightness' purpose;
Grinding awaits them after all,
O apostle grain, go on with thy mission.

41. Ode to Butterfly

O butterfly on the soft petals,
Flowers yellow of daffodil,
Its trumpet shaped central crown,
Dilute thou the bulb poisonous;
On cactus type pointed flowers,
And bright coloured in dahlia,
Perch upon daisy's disk floret,
Among white, purple petals,
Fly over dandelion's solitary flower,
Disperse its white haired seeds,
Create lonely smiles around.
Compromise lily's varieties many,
Its showy flowers purple,
Spotted golden, yellow and crimson,
Pure white, some with spots darker,
Thou cluster over each of them,
Flare also with lobes fragrant,
Hearty shape thine in cluster hued,
Match its leaves heart shaped,
Aid thus the florist trade,
Parent as you orchid flowers,
Siblings variety in shape, size, colour,
Thou but favour them all.

Too much colour hearted then,
Thou fly drunken, fluttering,
Take off as you from
Poppy's white, pink red cups,
Bell then tulip's bell shaped one,
Its bluish green leaves smile,
Pointed, they show colours ebrious.
Sweet scented nectar from
Garden violet makes you fly again,
Its central petal with guidelines
To pollinate, to procreate,
And thou further the nature there.
O highly coloured and patterned,
Flier strong, migrating distances great,
Thou nectar, plant juice feeder,
Wings rest vertically for short,
As thine club shaped antennae
Senses flowers from far.

42. A Flower in a Hermetically Sealed Prison

O destiny, why thou create flowers?
Why with thy destitutory powers
Thou hide thy sibilant voice?
Why the ultimate lot feigns as a choice?
O fate, why thy appointed lot
Comes with a lacy and gauzy coat?
Swinish hiss posing as a sing-song,
To undo and annihilate even hopes of long.
Why some people suffer so much?
Why, fatality tries to quench
Its thirst from the same well?
Why for some there is always a hell?
Perhaps, the invincible necessity
Has only thorns for some in its kitty,
Its purplish look of prey
Mind not the foundling's bray.
Aah, the fixed ruin
For the whitish fresh jasmine!
And the joy-hog with its filmy eyes,
Lapping heart amidst someone's cries.
Wild hilarity and wild rhythm
By fatality's doom to its fathom,

Why then a flower is born
If the spring is only but desert-lorn?

43. Ode to an Immortal Girl

What can death do to thee?
Thou, who's enlightened at this little age,
And approach it with a glee,
After such blessed souls death hast a futile chase.
For, people like thou only play with it,
Lay it worthless by fearing it not,
Only by people like thou it gets hit,
Immortal flowers, while, never get shot.
O thou, who makest time meaningless
By living infinitely in its every unit!
Instant any can't complain chancelessness,
Endless is thy journey without limit!
If a single instant can claim immortality,
And goodness pride in its agelessness,
Then thou but do them a duty,
Take them so far without any shiftiness.
Souls like thou are creator's manifestations,–
Harmony-fairy with its lullaby,
And a soothing voice to hurried steps to destinations,
How can we separate God from its baby?
Happily go, O angel, to that finest
Destination amidst heavens,

For the death will always fail in its quest,
As thou personify His sermons.

44. Rhyme's First Day

Today is the 1st of January,
The day as if in love,
Black-silvery, it says sorry
To the cloud-veiled sun's shove.
A new day with a new aurora,
Week new with new lyre,
20th gone, now 21st opera,
And millennium new with aurum-aureola.
Yes! New Year's first day
With its rainy ray.
Droplets with winy chorus falling,
Ebriated, chilly air goes sailing.
And we get an excited shiver,
Like a river
In a cold rainy vale;—
New drink for humanity's hail.
Trees dance to a moderate gale,
Leaves rustle to rainy tune,
Pouring as destiny's boon—
A new day too in some solitary dale.
The cold, wet new day,
Still with an aeonic silvery new ray,
Flaura fauna make hay,

Like a wave enters a new bay.

45. Rhyme's Last Day

The year prepares to say bye,
Here comes the last day with a sigh:
'Pray I for the humanity's high',
Takes birth the 366th with a cry,
The dawn having a sunny try
Over the mist which lie
Silvery still around His 'eye',
Which struggle against the eyed sly.
O new rays upon facets awry,
Would'u make them diamonds? 'Ay'
Says the day's eye,
Oh! The eye from the sky,
Ponder over earthling's vie.
From the time gone by
Gods doth fly
On chariot rays, to lay by
Godhood and get terrestrial tie.
O Dawn, thou doth imply,
Pious start for all and I,
Say as thou a smiling 'hi'
To the love hungry; lover's eye,
And the obstacles face a 'why'
As thou hand over a gyve

For the fates dry.
Thy sunny camp; tight up a guy,
New delicacies thou fry
For the bellies where even the hunger die.
Day, thou handling a key,
To bring fatality to its knee.

46. Dyad, Reality Never

We smiled, dulcified with
Great display: the life song,
But alas! Eburine years passed,
Crony days ebbed, never to come again.
Crowned each other, thought
Two paths always go parallel,
But, we just tread side by side,
Only to slip away, at the opportunity first.
Blame not friend or thyself,
As we are 'friends at court',
It is a day, dawn to dusk;
We meet only to drift away.
Inevitable as it is, humans
Beat never the dust same;
All need own track,
Runs where nobody besides.
O man! Crib not about vaporous friendliness lost,
Never judge friendship by time,
Feeds it only on the present; future preys,
So, cherish only moments those.

47. Mysterious End of a Song

Life is a song,
Which soul singths;
The spirit playing matter's lyre,
Melody starting with first cry,
Goes on and on,
Till completion of the journey,—
Notes high and notes low;
Beats ecstatic and tragic most;
Sometimes fast and sometimes pensively slow,
The soul goes on playing
The strings in body's harp,
And then the barely audible;
The last twinge at the death bed,
The soul as if in a hurry,
Plays the mysterious rhythm,
Which, though, completion of the song,
Stands distinct for its abstractness.
Aah! Why is it that
Most of the songs end on a tragic note?
Why not the escaping soul,
Plays the most rhythmic tone
At that moment last?

Consoles which those eyes
Where pain creates furious storms.

48. The Farmer and the Night

The night was spiritually lit; milky,
Aha such a beautiful night!
But, still not lucky
To dazzle in a couple's love delight.
Perhaps, alone with its misty milky light,
Hey Look! A farmer is there,
Irrigating his wheatlings amidst frosty bite,—
Ritual holiest by this agrestic seer.
And water here or there shines
To a chilly chide by the moon,
While, milky loneliness pines
For its brave son a harvest boon.
His feet numb in freezing water,
Amidst 'warmly sleepers' he seems a martyr.

49. Where's Love Gone

O gem, why thou shone
Lovely in my eyes?
Why thou were born of aeon,
If beauty's reflection surely dies?
Even memories have gone
To the deepest burial,
Faintest memories sometimes moan
Over the love's funeral.
Why they say
That love never dies?
It, of course, does on the dooms day,
When someone so lovely, heavenwards flies.
What is the use of fragrant shower?
If you do not see the flower!

50. Rhyme's Crime

Aah, the era of hard talk!
Each and everybody vies for
The worldly stretch across the pages,
Depict which paged humanity;
Words, only words, queuing
Along the social misdeeds,
Still, each counts for millions!
Alas! The soft talk;
The words which lit up
Invisible illumination over superficiality,
The language which only
A flower can sense,
So few words!
Still, saying the epic tale
Of humanity's glory,
But, they fetch nothing.
Perhaps, the soft talkers have
The sixth sense,
Enables which the common five
To mix up and come out
As an apostle of reality,
Understands which nobody.
Why then a bard should create a rhyme,

If all dump it as an economic crime?

51. A Newborn in a Himalayan Cave

A *sanyasi* in the cave,
Where the Himalayas pave
The highest path; stony silence rave
Rhymes musical, as Ganga brave
Boulders, which gave
Into the ascetic wave.
And his beard grows
Like the flora unchecked across
The edgy vale; happy of course:
Who lovest not cravings loss?
And there sits the man; legs cross,
Static they forget dashy furrows.
The rain when drips
Through the roof, perhaps to frisk
The human through trips,
Urvashi but fails in its tricks,
Him, the stone, Ganga's monotony grips,
For billion faiths, prayer only lips.
Comes when the sun,
Or the day at its final run,
He perceives not the job done,
And the fauna making fun

Leaves him as if none,
Who knows? Maybe with some pun!
This child in mighty father's womb,
His soul chants 'Om. Om. Om................'
Delivered once by mom,
Now the second through father's dome
To a world ebriated with *Som.*
And where souls freely roam.

52. Moony Mother's Light

Look how the night milks
The whole landscape spread infantly,
Like a mother breastfeeding her child gently,
And everything hazy eyed by winy maternal sips,
Vow! O moony night thy motherly lips
Kiss the sleepy panorama; the mother saintly
Strokes everything lying in her lap faintly,
O sleepless mother thy head never trips!
Look how whitish the love bathes the shadows!
Aura such that even ghosts seem friendly,
What fear has to do near love such,
Thus, every soul opens all its windows,
So that mother's light enter grandly,
And still she never finds it too much!

53. Ode to the Autumn

Autumn, thou stand betwix
The summer and the winter,
Still, like divinity thou mix
Contradictions: The soul and the matter.
Summer still warms during the day,
As, takes it paddy to its youth,
Winter too sneaks in after the sun's last ray,—
Dew almost rains to water their mouth.
Summer's last ripening and windfall;
Last gift to that lonely little lass,
Looking eagerly into some tree tall,
'What'd I offer', the winter guess.
Autumn, thou save that farmer from weather bite,
Which the two extremities try to force by fight.

54. Puzzled Summer

Wispy summer bides a hesitating bye,
As nature's law forces exile
To the other hemisphere, along Nile,
Awaits which eagerly hot fairy's sigh,
That tropical ever-greenery doth wry
Over the cool lover gone vile;—
Makest love too much in spring's guile,
Over-bred, she calls thou with a cry.
Thou but autumn-stricken here:
Pine for these dew rainy nights
Over the winter flowers already sown,
Like a mother thou fear
Warmly for children left alone in cold's delights,
And with a fleecy sob thou moan.

55. The Immortal Eating Mortality

Death, when thou'll come,
I don't know how'd I feel,
O thou destroyer of life's zeal,
Thou keep perfect mum,
So many noises fall upon thy ears dumb,
Thus, nobody knows how to deal
With the deaf host gulping last meal;
Listening not to prayers and Godly hymn.
O thou majestic unknown hunter,
So certain is thy grip on the prey
That lifelong we prepare ourselves as food thine,
And thou quickly saunter
Over the eyes with last ray,
Death, how you'd stamp mortality mine?

56. Little Morning Star

Little houri! When I saw
Thou for the first,—
Morning star in the horizon east,
Fought which night's awe,
To change my morning's law.
And there I was standing wonderstruck,
Pondering, now when sky has been recast,
Dost this new star takes row
To shine for me during the day?
Sun's light I have'd enough,
What dost this new celestial angel creates?
There I was cajoling my new ray,
The lips parted for a laugh;
O my ears, what heaven narrates?

57. To the Spring Bygone

Summer hast arrived
As all the spring flowers begone;
When so many smiles shone,
Sun brighter now; perfume fried :
Flowery dust lie buried,
Small whiff and even that gone;
Scented maiden's ashes thrown,
Sis's dusty reaches get seed.
Silver Goddess sweetly hiss
Upon everything from leaves to tongues:
Dry leaves' short sway;
Discharmed lips open to kiss
The lost perfumed songs;—
Spring doth seem so far away.

58. The Ever Flying Kite

See the kite's sway in the sky:
Papered soul pulls for escaping fly,
Corded attachment but to the earthly;—
The life force to its limits finally.
The will of the soul for free float,
Alas! Possible only jerks lot,
Till the last drop hot,
The instinct, the desire leaves not.
And the momentary penury released,
As if to get the prisoner appeased,
What a beggar the besieged!
Pious but still teased.
Yes, broken at last! That wondrous free flight,
Alas but until fall for earthly delight.

59. The Winner Takes it All

There walks the winner; triumphant
Shine of sweat on the brow,
Once he almost gave up, now buoyant
Bosom swells solid for the morrow.
There is the loser's bent head,—
Eyes which once sparkled, dropped dead;
Unnoticed, uncared to destiny's glad;
Bosom hunched back and example bad.
Who makes this greatest loss?
The difference between winning and losing,
Is it deciding time's momentary chaos?
Or those long hours found no time moving.
Branded two species; unmatching,
Aah! That even after single hatching.

60. Aha, That Moment!

Aha that contemplative inward time!
Body when reaches its prime;
In harmony with mind, writes a rhyme,
Illusions not, but reality shine.
Aha that divine perfect position!
No couple ever found such satisfaction,
Every part stimulates loveliest reaction,—
Soul sends such vibration.
Aha that obliviousness to deflected reality;
Self-truths forced for social duty,
This but is the true beauty,
Simple, straight without sociality.
Aha that becoming part of the whole!
Where individual plays no role,—
Still, a huge stage with character sole,
And that possibility with single pole.
Aha that sudden cosmic struck!
When the ultimate crisply lurk,
And falsely hard-worked walls jerk,
Transform these into heavenly arc.
Aha that golden light inside head!
Beats which the dark dead,
Infinite facets cut the fad

To a glittering diamond on something dead.
Aha that helplessness of senses!
Struck which through the tenses,
Come they now across the fences,
Liberate which infinity in His ranches.
Aha that time of being with the being!
And seeing too much without seeing,
Crowning moment of the body's king;
Yes! Soul triumphant, possessively sing.

61. On Intimacy with Mysterious Moment

Had I known the time
When the sleep came
Over me like the name;
Thou great mystery infinite!
With that instant to ignite,
I could light a small rhyme:
First maiden to be kissed firstly,
Or, ye lightening sky briskly
To quench the thirst of yore
Eagerly awaiting the first downpour.
Me doth but fail,
Like a disappointed lover hail
The start of love days:
Gaze first, first meet,—
Time caught in crazy ways,
Again but sadness beat
Its unlyrical, unrhymed tomber,
Lost is that instant
In noise huge of the bomber.

62. Summer Flower

I was born on this day,
Quarter century old,
Time's scythe takes hold
Around years, months on the 5th May,
And the hot summer pay
For the cake gold,
Lies which in barn to be sold,
While sandy swirls make hay.
Thank thee O summer,
Only thou show passion for the child;
Arriving like the flower late,
Becomes who then a dreamer,—
Summer flower; without singlest trace wild,
Oh! The flower with unflowery fate!

63. Tauji

While the world was lost
in the frenzied tunes of urban lark,
In the countryside a faint flicker was
tiptoeing through the dark,
Slowly-slowly the torch
burnt high and bright,
Dynamic dimensions of its raylets
woke up the slumberous masses for a fight.
Dignified confidence and exalted impulse
of light went flinging forth,
Historically harassed and exploited millions
got fresh hopes in south and north,
Lo! The fringe folks arrived
at the forefront,
As the brightest star of Haryana
in the sky brightly burnt.
Tauji, how high and mighty thou were!
Still so down to earth and simple!
Corpulent informality thine
brought always a smiling dimple
On every face tormented by
a worrying wrinkle.
Thy simple soul,

Always solemnly cuddled into
the paternal throes of composing
lushly-lustrous future
for each and every one of us,
And when the brightest son of Haryana
was gone for the eternal sleep,
A scar was created incalculably deep,
While our helpless sky
fell into a mourning hush.
Still, O Tauji!
Thy steady and unvacillating goodness,
And that persistently pronounced forthrightness
will always remain with us
to guide us clear of every trouble's crush,
Thy enlightening sagaciousness,
And the robust bravado of your heart
will continue to inspire new green
sprouts in land troubled by thirst.
How fulsome was your love
for the common people!
How refreshing was your smile's verve!
Temper so gracefully proportioned
and enchantingly simple!
How immensely foreseeable
was character yours!
Just like a path straight
and an open book of pleasant hours,–

Without any twists and turns,
O Tauji great!
Thy large-hearted liberality
was simply unbelievable,
Sacrificed the Nation's highest post
without tiniest trace of grumble,
Now, others follow thy legendary step
and reap the political fruit,
But alas, hear they not
the cries of masses mute.
Who can forget
the old-age pension,
Aha, an enormously elaborate
example of public work!
Gone was crippling old's tension;
Rhythmically gleaming smiles now lurk.
O thou farmers' *messiah*!
You tactfully removed
the noose of debt from their neck,
Gave then a
fatherly pat on the back,
And they – helplessly hemmed in by
the merciless loops of modern banking –
found utmost solace
in thy patronage loop,
Heavily indebted backs with a droop
got straightened with pride,

Launched thou then
a new tirade against hunger,
New hopes now linger
in peasants' dry eyes of yore,
Opened as thou a new door
to pride and prosperity.
Mystic subtlety and exuberance
of thy demeanour,
And freely elaborate freedom
of the 'human' in you,
Reach O subjects at the King's
threshold at any hour,–
Aha, no officially reprimanding queue!
Your legacy burning
like a lamp
in stillest of silence,
And thy charisma holding
in spellbinding balance,
While time's arms
swinging helplessly and silently,
Grows as the great man's
legend almost exponentially,
Continue it will to
shine as our path's light,
And we the sturdy sons
will toil to reach the height
where you wanted us to reach–

A new, fighting determination
in heart each;
To get the justice
for everybody wronged;
A new prosperity in homes
where it never belonged;
For the youths a fresh start;
Evolve we'll a new art,
Whereby everything is in
exquisitely fine-proportioned
parallel to your cause,
Brethren! Let us prove our gratitude
to the man who brought
in teary eyes a smiling rose.
Long live our
grand spellbinder's legacy!
God! Let it perpetually
cut the time's fabric mazy!

Printed by Libri Plureos GmbH in Hamburg,
Germany